HEART
OF
HEARTS

CLAIRE ELIZABETH GROSE

Copyright © 2025 by Claire Elizabeth Grose

Compiled and edited by Michael Grose and June Kennedy

All rights reserved. No portion of this publication may be reproduced, stored in a retrieval system or transmitted in any form by any means – electronic, mechanical, photocopying, recording, or any other –except for brief quotation in printed reviews, without the prior written permission of the publisher.

Unless indicated otherwise, all scripture quotations in this book are from the following source:

The Good News Bible: The Bible in Today's English Version (TEV) © 1976 by the American Bible Society. Used with permission.

ISBN 978-0-6459888-5-7

Author contact information - clairegrose.heartmatters@gmail.com

Version 1.0

DEDICATION

This book is dedicated to my Saviour,
The Lord Jesus Christ, King of Kings, Lord of Lords,
Almighty God, Prince of Peace, the King of Glory.

CONTENTS

DEDICATION	IV
CONTENTS	V
PREFACE	VIII
ACKNOWLEDGEMENTS	X
PART ONE	1
MY DAILY PRAYER	4
HEAVEN'S BRIGHTEST STAR	5
THE LORD'S RADIANCE	6
DIVINE HOLINESS	7
MY BELOVED	8
FOREVER YOUNG	9
ALWAYS AND FOREVER	10
SIDE BY SIDE	11
MISTY MOON	14
DINNER FOR TWO	15
DAYS OF GOLD	16
ENCOUNTER GOD	17
THE HEART IS RIPE	18
HARMONY OF HEART AND MIND	19
HIS SWEETNESS WILL REMAIN	20
BUDS IN TIME	21
MORNING FOG	22
PERFECT PEACE	23
GOD'S TAPESTRY	26
WINGS OF FAITH	27
MY POURING PEN	28
ANGELS ON EARTH	29
PART TWO	30
JESUS PASSING BY TODAY	33
HIS GLORIOUS LIGHT	34
BE A POWERHOUSE FOR GOD	35
WINDS OF PEACE	36

WEALTH IN YOUR WORD	37
GOD'S PLAN IS ON THE RUN	38
A THREAD OF BELONGING	41
TODAY WE HAVE JESUS	42
THE GRANDEUR OF OUR LOVE	43
MY LIFEBUOY	44
SILENT CONVERSATION	45
SOUL TIME	46
LAMB OF GOD	49
GOD'S KNOWLEDGE AND WISDOM	50
YOUR WORD	51
MOMENT OF CONFESSION	52
SPIRIT WORDS	53
AGELESS TIME	54
THE OPEN SPIRIT HEART	57
HEART MATTERS	58
ONE IN THREE; THE TRINITY	59
THE HEART OF GOD	60
THERE'S WORK TO DO	61
VOICES IN THE SILENCE	62
THE BEST IS YET TO COME	63
IN PERFECT COMMUNION	64
KING OF MERCY	65
EVERY DAY IS A NEW PAGE	66
WHEN GOD MOVES THE SOUL	67
MY JESUS	68
PART THREE	69
THE SPIRIT HEART	72
QUIET TIME TOGETHER	73
LIVING WATERS	74
REVELATION BREAKTHROUGH	75
YOUR SPIRIT IN ME LORD	76
PASSING THROUGH	77
MAKEOVER	80
PEARLS OF LIGHT	81

THE VOICE IN ME *82*
UNTARNISHED LOVE *83*
THE FIRST HOLY SEED... *84*
A LONGING IN THE HEART *85*
PART FOUR *86*
IN THE SHADOWS OF GETHSEMANE *89*
ABSOLUTION *90*
IN THE SHADOWS OF THE OLIVE GROVE *91*
REUNION... *94*
GOOD ENOUGH FOR A PARDON *95*
NEW BORN KING... *98*
IN AWE SHE HELD HIM.. *99*
MESSIAH BORN IN THE STABLE.. *100*
A PRICELESS LIFE *101*

PREFACE

Two things I just wanted to say about this book are, why I started writing and how I came by the title.

I grew up in the 1950's-1960's in Adelaide, South Australia, my life was pretty simple but wonderful. I was very lucky to have a secure family life, and my Mum and Dad brought the family up to treat others with respect, do the right thing, be courteous, and respect your elders. We had a strict upbringing and even as adults our parents never criticized us but encouraged us to do our best in life. They were "Aussie battlers" but we always managed to make it through the tough times!

They were people of integrity and cared about others and instilled that into our family.

Church was a big part of our lives growing up. We went to Sunday School at an early age and progressed up through the appropriate groups as we got older.

Youth groups, camps and church anniversaries were all important to the whole family. We competed in church sports teams, basketball and tennis with other parishes across Adelaide. Life-long friendships were in the making and cherished golden memories to look back on that would never fade.

Bible stories, hymns and choruses were all part of getting to know Jesus. This nurturing finally led me to the day Jesus came knocking on my heart's door. Being filled with the Holy Spirit is something I will never forget and the overwhelming power of His love that filled my whole being and propelled me to the front of the hall to give my heart to Him. No words can fully describe the joy I felt. That was in February 1968, I was 14 years of age. He has been my Shining Light ever since, and lives within me always.

So I thank my beautiful Mum and Dad for the way they raised me and for the foundation of knowing Jesus' love.

It was in His love that I started to write, in the Autumn of 1993. My journey has brought me to this book "Heart of Hearts", my 15th book. I wanted to share my favourite poems that fill my heart with joy and a knowing that He is who He says He is through His Word and His heart can love the whole wide world!

My own "God revelation" when I was 14 years old has revealed His wondrous love to me and the heart changing experience through His gift of the Holy Spirit, who dwells in the heart of every believer in Jesus.

The Lord watches over our hearts, "Peace is what I leave with you; it is my own peace that I give you. I do not give it as the world does. Do not be worried and upset; do not be afraid."

John 14:27 Good News Bible.

When I was a young Christian reading my Bible was really important to me in getting to know Jesus as my personal Saviour and became the foundation that I built my faith on.

It gave me strength and courage as I began life in the workforce at the age of 16. Coming from a sheltered upbringing it was my life-line to self-confidence and adapting to social life at work.
The poems reflect the everyday feelings and emotions that we feel as we meet the challenges of life and how the great magnitude of God's love can help us rise above them.

Many of these writings have been my first words of whispered prayer, so much that I have been moved to write them down at once and continue on in His wonderful and absolute love.

Together we write as He provides my inspiration.

All glory to Him, my precious Lord Jesus!

ACKNOWLEDGEMENTS

My heartfelt thanks to my beloved family, my Mum and Dad, Lilly and Ken, and my siblings Jeanette, June, Carol, Gloria and Lynne, for their never ending encouragement and support to me. To the rest of the family, you are all a precious link that joins us together.

To Michael and Andrew for your continual support to me in fulfilling my passion of writing poems for the Lord to help others through His Word.

A huge thank you to Junie for editing my poems and the coffees and lunches we enjoyed along the way.

To Joy Furnell for her Crown of Thorns drawing, you have an amazing gift, thank you Joy.

A special thank you to Salisbury Uniting Church, Adelaide for photos. Used by permission.

A big thank you to Carol and Dennis, Lynne and Joshua Woskett for great photos. Also thank you Den for the Fishes and Loaves Reflection photo, taken in Jerusalem.

To my friends and Church Families, thank you for your love and support.

To my beautiful sons, Michael and Andrew, and your families. Thank you for loving me, and I am so glad He gave you to me. I cherish my grandchildren, I love you all so much.

To you the reader, thank you for picking this book up and I pray you will find His peace and love on the pages ahead.

May He shower you all with His love and blessings.

PART ONE

"Then Moses requested, "Please let me see the dazzling light of your presence." The Lord answered, "I will make all my splendour pass before you and in your presence I will pronounce my sacred name"...

Exodus 33 : 18, 19

HEART OF HEARTS

JESUS IS SACRED...
ALL DIVINE, MAJESTY AND POWER...

"I, Jesus, have sent my angel to announce these things to you in the churches. I am descended from the family of David; I am the bright morning star."
"The Spirit and the Bride say, "Come!""

Revelation 22 : 16, 17

MY DAILY PRAYER

Be with me, stay with me,
Close by my side,
Fill me with Your peace and love,
So my spirit shall surely fly
To the heights in Your love,
As only You can give,
Prepare me for this day ahead,
So in me You'll always live.

HEAVEN'S BRIGHTEST STAR

Beautiful One, that's You Lord
You supply my every need,
I only have to think of You,
You grant me peace indeed.

Your presence I can feel,
It's only a breath away,
I feel You close right next to me,
That's where You'll always stay.

Heaven's brightest star, that's You,
Your beauty is all around,
From snowflake to mountain view,
Your glory can be found.

Heaven's brightest star, that's You,
You want me just as I am,
You will change me in Your Light
So I can be the best I can.

Heaven's brightest star,
Where crystal waters flow,
Your Crown of Light shines bright,
You are seated on Your Throne.

Heaven's brightest star,
For all Eternity,
You are the Lamb of God,
You bring me to my knees.

THE LORD'S RADIANCE

Lord, Your radiance is so bright,
Only spirit eyes can see,
Your glory in great magnitude,
I can only imagine Thee.

Your radiance so powerful
With a million beams,
Filled with rainbow prisms
Is what I conceive to be.

You are the Almighty,
Everlasting God of Heaven and Earth,
Your radiance shines forever
In Your Kingdom that was the first.

Your radiance so healing,
More than a hundred suns,
Your warmth and balm will soothe
The generations to come.

Yes, Your radiance precious Jesus,
Son of the Holy Trinity,
We can live in Your glory,
We only have to "believe".

DIVINE HOLINESS

The Holy Trinity, Divine Holiness
You sit on Your Throne,
In majesty and splendour
One day will call us home.

Your glory is transcendent,
Holy in every way,
A beauty sublime,
Takes our breath away.

Your Divine Holiness
Exceeds wonder and joy,
Beyond our comprehension
You are Magnificence and Awe.

On the day You return
We will see the Glorified You,
A vision overwhelming
Mankind renewed.

Divine Holiness; The Groom and His Church,
One day will be revealed
When we meet the Saviour,
Our destiny fulfilled.

Divine Holiness;
One day will claim the soul,
To take its place in Eternity
Where we are made whole.

MY BELOVED

"You are my beloved", says the Lord
"I crave to know you more,
Come to Me for everything
Because it's you I adore."

"You were made in My image,
I love you as My own,
I call you My Sons and Daughters,
In Heaven I've prepared your home."

"You are My beloved,
I forgave you long ago,
I bore the Cross for you,
I can never let you go."

"I long for your acceptance
To believe I died for you,
Your sin I remember no more,
My Father raised Me out of the Tomb."

"So come to Me, My beloved,
My glory will never end,
I have blessings untold,
That everyday to you I send."

"I sit beside The Father in Heaven
But I sent My Spirit to you,
One day I will return
To bring you home above the blue."

FOREVER YOUNG

Forever young lives in Eternity,
The old is made new,
The repented heart now rewarded
With the gifts Christ has for you.

No signs of pain or struggles,
The victor is set free,
Forever young in Paradise
Because on earth you believed.

Forever young knows the Risen Lord,
A surrendered vow brought Paradise,
Your eternal journey now leaves you
With standing room at His side.

His sparkling Throne lies before you,
The King of Glory in splendour abides,
And the "Ancient of Days"; Holy Father,
Together they sit side by side.

Angels roar in their presence
And sing in worship sweet,
With adoration they lowly bow
At His Pierced Feet.

Forever young made whole,
Perfection by His Pierced Hands,
The throngs of Heaven never cease
To worship the Holy Lamb!

ALWAYS AND FOREVER

Always and forever Lord
You will be the great "I Am",
Truth and grace Your stronghold
Because You are the Holy Lamb.

You were born in a stable
On the holiest of nights,
Always and forever Lord
You wear the Crown of Life.

Always and forever Lord
You will love the whole wide world,
Your mission is to save us,
Your message we must tell.

Always and forever Lord
You are the Risen Christ
Your hands and feet bore the nails
So we could have eternal life.

You gave us Your Holy Spirit,
Holy is Your Name,
Always and forever Lord
Blessed: You remain.

SIDE BY SIDE

You are my lifeline
When I'm weak or strong,
When I'm happy or sad
Side by side we belong.

You are my life line
Whether I'm young or old,
To You it makes no difference
As long as I'm one of Your fold.

You are my life line
You supply my needs,
That You already know
Before I ask for these!

You are my life line,
Side by side we'll always stay
Your power and your glory
Will surround me day by day.

Yes, side by side we belong
For all eternity,
In spirit and in truth
I will see Your victory.

HEART OF HEARTS

OUR GOD …
OUR CREATOR…

"…His splendour covers the heavens, and the earth is full of his praise. He comes with the brightness of lightning; light flashes from his hand, there where his power is hidden."

Habakkuk 3 : 3, 4

MISTY MOON

Misty moon in the sky
On a winter's night,
Waiting for the haze to pass
To shine her light so bright.

Softly she hangs up there
To mark the end of day,
Stars begin to shine,
We see the Milky Way.

Misty moon sits patiently
To pass the night away,
Designed by the Saviour
He sends her on her way.

Misty moon so perfect,
His Light for the night,
Misty moon God's wonder,
Amongst the stars so bright.

Misty moon so silent
Still speaks a thousand words,
Melts my heart completely
When she shows her perfect curves.

DINNER FOR TWO

I long to see You standing
Before my eyes tonight,
Then dear, dear Lord
Everything would be alright.

To serve You at my table
The best of the best,
So we could eat together
And the food You would bless.

The finest wine I could find,
Is there any fit for the King?
To pass Your lips of wonder
That spoke to stop the wind!

And conversation, what would we say?
To pass the time while we eat,
I think the contents of my heart
I would lay at Your feet.

And the candle light would shine
In Your eyes full of love
As they held my gaze completely,
You are the Son of God.

But through faith I see You now
And feel Your love divine,
That's how it is for the present
While I wait until my time.

DAYS OF GOLD

The day is fresh,
I come into Your presence,
I praise and worship You Lord,
The God of Heaven.

I feel Your embrace,
Refreshed and restored,
Because of Your Spirit
I adore You Lord.

I have come full circle
In my walk with You,
The lessons I have learnt,
I feel renewed.

The days of youth,
Treasured memories I hold,
Through Your Spirit so close,
I now live in days of gold.

Shadows once real,
Days of gold have erased,
As I journey with Your Spirit
All the rest of my days.

Your gift of The Spirit Lord
So precious to behold,
Sent down by The Father,
I now live in days of gold.

ENCOUNTER GOD

Encounter God,
Bring your thoughts to rest,
Be still in His presence,
The silent, unseen guest!

Encounter God,
In the hush of day
Listen for His voice,
He longs for you today.

Wait at His Throne,
Share your deepest care,
He's thrilled with your victory
Because a kind word you shared.

Encounter God,
Make your life worthwhile,
His Sacrifice made you special,
Will you go the extra mile?

Encounter God,
Learn His Ways and Words,
An awakening of His power
Because your heart His Spirit stirred!

THE HEART IS RIPE

The Holy Spirit's touch
Will bring you to your knees,
A holy moment
Face to face with Thee.

The heart is ripe,
Surrendering all inside,
The soul full of humility
With tears you just can't hide.

Nothing else in the world
Matters right now,
An anointing from The Spirit
Leads you to a vow.

An overwhelming feeling,
Thoughts are quiet inside,
The heart is full,
An endowment from The Most High.

The heart is ripe
For the Fruits of The Spirit,
A cleansing takes place,
His voice you now hear it.

When the heart is ripe
You kneel at the Seat of His Throne,
A humble revelation,
He now calls you His own.

HARMONY OF HEART AND MIND

When the heart is full of God's love
The mind is filled with peace,
An awakening of His Spirit
Now harmony is released.

They respond together
Like the moon with the tide,
In God's perfect union
The harmony of heart and mind.

An awakening of The Spirit,
Washes you clean to refresh,
Now feeling overwhelmed
Your heart wants to repent.

The harmony of heart and mind
Like First Light and Morning Song,
So sweet to the Christian heart
For you the Saviour longs.

When the heart and mind blend together
Like the chords of a tune,
Sweet fragrance seems to rise
Now you are renewed.

The harmony of heart and mind
Blend together like the Dawn and Dusk,
Union of Father and Son,
Bow to them we must.

HIS SWEETNESS WILL REMAIN

His sweetness will flow over you
In streams of golden light,
Drifting through your heart
To make you shine so bright.

His love so divine
Will wash you white as snow,
His sweetness will remain
If you make it so.

Like the sweetness of Spring
Refreshing to the soul,
New life will awake,
Inner changes will take hold.

His blessings will flow
In never ending gifts,
His sweetness will remain
Because you are His.

Put Him first in your life,
Commit each day to Him,
His sweetness will remain,
His Spirit will live within.

God of Glory forever,
His sweetness will remain,
Every knee will bow,
Holy is His Name.

BUDS IN TIME

We are but buds in time
As we grow in His love divine,
Speaking to the soul within,
We only have to look to Him.

To feel the comfort of His open arms
And to receive His blessings of peace and calm,
We only have to ask for these gifts
That will lead us to eternal bliss.

So like the sweet bud on the vine
Responds to the warmth of daily sunshine,
Grows into a beautiful bloom,
Our faith will blossom if we give Him room!

MORNING FOG

Quiet bliss as fog rolls in
Covering sea and land,
Profound peace fills my soul
As I stand on dampened sand.

Thoughts are lost in the haze
As landscape becomes a blur,
Lapping ripples pat the shore
The only sound to be heard.

Landmarks are out of view
From the fog that's hanging still,
Sun does its best to shine
But through the fog it never will.

Shells embedded in the sand
That the tide left far behind,
Waiting for its return
And the journey beyond the "blue line".

I just can't believe how surreal that moment was,
Standing on the beach in the morning fog,
Thank You Lord for this time and the peace that came to me
Just like it came to You, on the shores of Galilee.

PERFECT PEACE

Perfect peace is what I feel
When I trust in You,
My faith and love so strong,
It's all I need to do.

When I feel worried
And fear rises up,
I cling to You Lord,
God's own precious Son.

I have no doubt at all
That You will look after me,
In You I claim my prayer
Because of Calvary.

I have perfect peace,
Calmness I feel,
My trust in You secure,
My love for You so real.

Your Spirit brought Your peace to me,
He is Your precious gift,
I thank You Holy Father
Because in me He lives.

HEART OF HEARTS

IN PRAISE AND WORSHIP...
WE SING TO THE LIVING GOD...

"Praise him, sun and moon; praise him, shining stars.
Praise him, highest heavens, and the waters above the sky."

Psalm 148 : 3, 4

GOD'S TAPESTRY

God weaves His tapestry
Over Mother Earth,
Through the seasons that come
To change the face of her.

He makes windy roads
And snow capped peaks,
He weaves grassy fields,
Golden sunsets that speak.

He embroiders flowers
With fragrance so sweet,
The lilies of the fields
That make it so complete.

He weaves highs and lows
Over mountains and plains,
The streams and rivers
Running after rain.

His finest work is in our heart,
So complex and complete
Filled with His Spirit divine,
Only God could create such majesty!

WINGS OF FAITH

Use those wings of faith
As you go forward in His Light,
He's thrilled to see you welcome
His Word as you go through life.

Use those wings of faith
To rise above things untrue,
A testing time for many
Stand firm in His grace and truth.

Those wings of faith so strong,
Tossed about from earthly cares,
Everyday are renewed
As His Spirit performs repairs.

Wings of faith can withstand
The feelings of despair
But through His Holy Spirit
Your heart will know He is there.

Use those wings of faith
To refresh and restore,
By His Holy Word
He couldn't love you more.

Wings of faith will battle
Every crisis and fear,
Stretch those wings of faith
Let God come near.

MY POURING PEN

My pouring pen flows with His love,
A love that knows no end,
For all people of the world,
A love His Spirit sends.

My pouring pen flows anytime
And also anywhere,
Day or night it's with me,
His wondrous love I share.

I write His Words to the world
So they will receive His gift
To accept Him into their heart,
So forever they will live.

My pouring pen runs like a river
Sometimes fast, sometimes slow,
Be sure these words will come
From the Saviour who loves us so.

My pouring pen is for His lambs
And those who want to come,
His Kingdom is forever more
To receive God's only Son.

ANGELS ON EARTH

There are angels on Earth Lord
To do Your chosen work,
To help with a special need
Because You were the First.

The First to show us how to love,
To give a helping hand,
That's why there are angels on Earth
Who make Your Holy stand.

There are angels on Earth
Who go the extra mile,
To bridge the gap of hopelessness,
To meet a need worthwhile.

There are angels on Earth Lord
Who display Your heavenly love,
Your very faithful servants
Bring hope from You above.

So thank You Lord, for Your angels on Earth
Who love so endlessly,
You charge them with Your power,
To bring us close to Thee.

PART TWO

"…Jesus took with him Peter, James, and John, and led them up a high mountain, where they were alone. As they looked on, a change came over Jesus, and his clothes became shining white…"

Mark 9 : 2, 3

HEART OF HEARTS

OPEN YOUR HEART'S DOOR...
TO HIS ETERNAL LOVE...

"Listen! I stand at the door and knock; if anyone hears my voice and opens the door, I will come into his house and eat with him, and he will eat with me.."

Revelation 3 : 20

JESUS PASSING BY TODAY

Imagine the frenzy
If Jesus passed by today,
Walking down your street
And through your gate He came.

He stands at your door
Knocking so gently,
A quiet voice says
"My Father sent me."

"Your sin I remember no more,
I was crucified at Calvary,
Stranger, I suffered the nails
So you could live with me."

Will you be silent
As His eyes hold your gaze?
Will you follow Him?
He's passing by today!

Will He win your heart
So you can live forever with Him,
When Jesus comes by today
Will you let Him in?

Yes, He loves you so dearly,
Will you let Him in
When He knocks at your door?
So your Eternity can begin.

HIS GLORIOUS LIGHT

His glorious light will shine
On every heart that gives Him room,
When you turn to Him
He will heal your deepest wound.

His glorious light a beacon
For the lost to find their way,
Hope and forgiveness He offers,
On your heart He will lay.

His glorious light will bring
A love that will never part,
His anointing balm so sweet,
He will pour into your heart.

So let His glorious light
Shroud you wherever you are,
Take His Hand of Mercy,
You will shine like the Evening Star.

BE A POWERHOUSE FOR GOD

Every faithful soul who dwells
Beneath the arms of Christ,
Becomes a powerhouse within
For His love to shine so bright.

Shining on the inside
Lord Your love will never stop,
Where Your Holy Spirit lives
We are a powerhouse for God.

Our chores are never done
Because we try to answer Your call,
Lord Your love burns so brightly
To sustain us if we fall.

Though we grow tired Lord,
Our strength You will revive,
Because we are a powerhouse
Our needs You will supply.

Challenges come along
But it's Your power we need,
We only have to ask,
By Your will we can succeed.

So be a powerhouse for God,
You will see Eternity,
He will charge you with His power,
You will rise to victory.

WINDS OF PEACE

Holy Spirit come
With Your winds of peace,
Restore my soul,
Let my heart breathe.

I need Your healing power
To flow over me,
Like the ebb of the tide
That will never cease.

Come Holy Spirit,
May Your winds of peace
Fill my soul to overflow
And suffice the needs in me.

Hush the clamour
Of my whirling mind,
Bring Your winds of peace
So deliverance I find.

God's gift to earth,
Great Comforter You are,
You bring Your winds of peace
To restore the calm.

Come Holy Spirit,
Bring Your winds of peace
With Your majesty and power
From the Holy Trinity.

WEALTH IN YOUR WORD

There's wealth in Your Word Lord
Far beyond compare,
We only have to open it
And read what lies there.

There's wealth in Your Word Lord,
Comfort, healing and joy,
Always never ending,
At hand for us to deploy.

There's wisdom and knowledge
For direction and truth,
There's wealth in Your Word Lord
For us to read through.

Yesterday, today and tomorrow
Your Words will stay the same,
There's wealth in Your Word Lord
That will never fade.

Yes, there's wealth in Your Word Lord,
King of Glory You are,
One day You will return
To take us past the stars!

GOD'S PLAN IS ON THE RUN

On those days you feel lonely
Opportunities just don't come,
Keep your faith and fear not,
God's plan is on the run.

Put Him first in your life
For decisions to make,
In trust you will receive,
Though His time He will take.

If nothing seems to be happening,
He's giving you some space
To meet Him privately
So He can serve His mercy and grace.

He's waiting for your acceptance
To let His plan come to you,
Open your heart today
So He can come on through.

He will fill your life with wonder
As you surrender to Him,
God's plan is on the run,
Your doubts will soon seem dim.

No other plan will do,
His Will must come to pass,
His plan is on the run,
You only have to ask!

MY SHEPHERD...
GOES BEFORE ME...

"My sheep listen to my voice; I know them, and they follow me. I give them eternal life, and they shall never die. No one can snatch them away from me."

John 10 : 27, 28

A THREAD OF BELONGING

Lord, in Your peace and calm
I ponder my life,
A thread of belonging
Is what I find.

In those moments
I think of You,
My thread of belonging
Leads to You.

Your tender love
Beckons me on,
Though trials appear
You make me strong.

My thread of belonging
Is strengthened by Your Grace
That you give abundantly
To all who seek Your face.

A thread of faith
Will swell like a river
Flowing in His pure love
That will surely last forever.

A thread of belonging
Will never come loose,
It leads to the Saviour
Who lives for me and you.

TODAY WE HAVE JESUS

Yesterday is gone with the sunset,
Tomorrow waits for the dawn,
The future lies in His hands
Waiting to be born.

We can't change what happened yesterday
If regret is the call,
But today we have Jesus
Who will catch us when we fall.

We can learn from yesterday
With hope in our heart,
Because today with the Saviour
We can make a fresh start.

Yes, today we have Jesus
As the sun rises high,
He's waiting to help you
As the hours pass you by.

THE GRANDEUR OF OUR LOVE

When I look to the clouds
I feel Your love divine,
I give my heart to You Lord
Because You are mine.

Earth cannot spoil
The grandeur of our love,
That goes beyond the stars
To Your heaven above.

You loved me first Lord
Before I was born,
You placed me in my mother's womb,
Together we saw the first dawn.

You gave me gifts to bless
Those loved ones in my heart,
I feel them overflowing
From Your love I must impart.

The grandeur of our love Lord
Will see Eternity,
Precious King of Kings,
One day Your face I'll see.

MY LIFEBUOY

My lifebuoy is my Saviour
Ready for my call,
My Counsellor at all times
To whom I surrender my all.

My emotions are tossed about
By rough and turbulent seas,
But my lifebuoy is around me
To give stability.

Though challenges come along,
Sometimes too much to bear,
My lifebuoy never leaves me,
His strength will be there.

He will soothe the waves
And hush the howling wind,
Peace and calm will come
That the heart will feel within.

My lifebuoy can withstand
The deepest, darkest storm,
His outstretched hand is reaching
To open the come dawn.

Receive Him as your lifebuoy,
Eternal Saviour, King of Kings,
Take His gift of life
Because you are His everything.

SILENT CONVERSATION

In silent conversation Lord
My thoughts run to You,
Without a spoken word
That You already knew.

In silent conversation
You know my heart's desire,
Your plan will prevail
No matter what betides.

In silent conversation
No words are exchanged,
Your thoughts, my thoughts
Are linked like a chain.

In silent conversation
Your Words come to me,
I praise and worship You Lord,
In my heart You'll always be.

SOUL TIME

Soul time is quiet time,
I feel Your presence near,
My focus is on You,
I bring my cares and fears.

I find Your peace and calm
Deep within my soul,
Heavenly bliss I feel inside
Because You have made me whole.

So thank You Lord for soul time
When I focus on You above,
To cease my thoughts just for a while,
I come to You for love.

HEART OF HEARTS

HE IS OUR TOWER OF STRENGTH... SUPREME IN POWER AND GRACE...

"He appeared in human form, was shown to be right by the Spirit, and was seen by angels. He was preached among the nations, was believed in throughout the world, and was taken up to heaven."

1 Timothy 3 : 16

LAMB OF GOD

I bow before Your Throne of Gold
Where You sit for all to behold,
By the Father You reside in time
In Your Word it is told.

Lamb of God, Your Throne of Gold,
Heaven's Most High above,
So sacred and divine,
I worship You in Holy love.

Lamb of God, Your Throne of Gold,
In Your power and glory You reign,
Your angels bow down to worship You,
"Blessed" You remain.

My prayer for the world is to acknowledge You
The "Lamb of God" on Your Throne,
So they will have Eternal Life,
And make Your Throne their home.

GOD'S KNOWLEDGE AND WISDOM

God's knowledge and wisdom can be yours
When an honest request is made,
He will guide your right decision
Because from your heart it came.

His power and glory will shine on you
Because you acted in your faith,
There is no other way,
From His supply you can take.

You can be sure His plan will open
When you call on His wisdom today,
As you conceded to His will
That is the only way.

Yes, His knowledge and wisdom are yours,
When you claim it in His Name,
He loves you beyond words,
He will never change!

YOUR WORD

The glory of the Lord
Stills my soul,
Thoughts come to rest,
My heart feels whole.

Your Word makes me complete
As I ponder Your ways,
My understanding wavers
But in Your love I remain.

Your Word is my guide
When life baffles me,
Choices to make,
Help me to see.

When I read Your Word Lord
I praise Your Holy Name,
Because I'm Your child,
My heart has truly changed.

Your Word is You Lord,
Complete in every way,
Down through the ages Lord,
You will never change.

Your Word changes lives
And brings us to our knees,
Your salvation and redemption
Paid the price at Calvary.

MOMENT OF CONFESSION

Lord, in this moment of confession
I come before Your Throne,
My heart I lay open
Because my soul You own.

I bring to You
My heart felt cares,
In those moments of truth
I confess what lays there.

No barriers hold me back
In my heart of hearts,
Because You know the truth
I must make a fresh start.

Your Spirit dwells within me,
The most precious gift from You,
In this moment of confession
I surrender my all to You.

There are things in my life
That still grieve me so,
In this moment of confession
I can let them go!

Teach me Your ways Lord
So I can overcome my grief,
Through Your Holy Spirit
Who led me to believe!

SPIRIT WORDS

Lord, help me to wait before You
To hear Your Spirit Words,
That will fall into my heart
Silently unheard.

My soul will react
With warmth from love so deep
That will change me forever
At Your Mercy Seat.

Your Spirit Words will come
From Your heart that can love the world,
That forgives each broken promise
And picks up each one who fell.

You'll forgive the deepest blow
That mankind can deal,
Because of Calvary
Eternal Life revealed.

Your Spirit Words forever sound
Through the centuries of time,
Are heard by Your beloved
To share with all mankind.

AGELESS TIME

God's ageless time is perfect,
It unfolds at His behest,
There is a beginning
But there never is an end.

This age is pure,
One day we will understand,
Don't worry how to get there
For the Saviour will take your hand.

He will lead you by crystal waters
And down streets paved with gold,
His glory will shine everywhere
In His light for you to behold.

This age is eternal,
There's nothing you will lack,
All you need is Jesus,
There's no need to look back.

No earthly words can describe
The wonders of ageless time,
The Holy One is waiting
To show you Paradise!

HEART OF HEARTS

A HEART OF GOLD...
IS FULL OF SOUL...

"But I am like an olive tree growing in
the house of God; I trust in his
constant love forever and ever."

Psalm 52 : 8

THE OPEN SPIRIT HEART

The open Spirit heart knows peace,
The kind God's Spirit sends,
His love forever lasting
That will never end.

The open Spirit heart relies
Upon His Written Word,
In praise, prayer and worship
Because God's voice is heard.

In loving fellowship
The Spirit will abide
In every open heart
That welcomes Him inside.

The open Spirit heart knows contentment
For every challenge that comes,
A trust and faith so real
To help you overcome.

The open Spirit heart communes
With God Himself,
A never ending union
That makes His presence felt.

The open Spirit heart reveals
The Glory of God's love,
In union with His Spirit
Who came down from above.

HEART MATTERS

Ask the Lord for His loving care
When heart matters rule the day,
Place them in His hands,
Then go on your way.

He has your best interest at heart,
There's nothing He'd rather do,
Relax and enjoy your day,
He will help you see it through.

No matter how slight or complex
These heart matters become,
Give them all to the Saviour
In His time the answer will come.

Your heart matters are in His hands
He knows each one well,
You only have to ask Him,
He is by your side to help.

So refresh your heart matters today
With trust and faith in your soul,
His Pierced Hands will soothe them
Like the ancient days of old.

ONE IN THREE; THE TRINITY

One in Three; The Trinity,
Divine Kingship and Authority,
Serve us with their love
For all humanity.

Touching the open soul,
Waiting for it to respond
To Your heavenly touch,
From Your Spirit it comes.

Your anointing takes place
To change and cleanse the heart,
Your light shines within
With a love that will never depart.

Steeped in love divine
Your faith and trust will grow,
One in Three; The Trinity
Their love to you they'll show.

THE HEART OF GOD

His Spirit will live inside you,
He will prompt you to do your best,
His love surrounds your being,
While in His arms you find rest.

Having the heart of God,
No man can ever own,
Until he receives Eternity
The greatest gift you'll ever know!

Having the heart of God
Knows true, divine love,
Nothing on this earth
Can match the nature of God.

Having the heart of God
Means going the extra mile,
Being caring and kind
To make each day worthwhile.

Having the heart of God
Is to cast your cares,
To step out in faith
And believe He will answer your prayers.

The heart of God
Knows true humility,
In Him all things are possible,
You will rise to victory!

THERE'S WORK TO DO

Your glorious love Lord
Demands our all,
Our lessons are many
When we accept Your call.

There's work to do
To refresh the heart,
New ways to learn
As the old ones depart.

The Spirit comes close
With comfort to heal,
Some old ways still surface
But His presence is real.

He wants us to share
Every need every day,
So our cares will be lighter
As we go on our way.

The old ways will beckon
But it's the new ones we need,
With the Spirit's help
We will surely succeed.

There's work to do
With the new heart we own,
Filled with His grace
New seeds we will sow.

VOICES IN THE SILENCE

Voices in the silence Lord
Speak so loud to me,
It's then I turn to You,
Your love comes tenderly.

Your promise I can stand on
For solace in my heart,
As I make a new beginning
On a different path.

The voices in the silence,
You can hush them all,
Your living Word I open
Gives me strength to stand tall.

My weakness I surrender,
I lay at the foot of Your Cross,
You gave Your life for me,
Now I'm not the person I was.

Your forgiveness lasts forever
And Your love goes past the beyond,
Give me Your grace and mercy,
Show me where I belong.

The voices in the silence Lord
You can change to angel chants,
Healing balm pours over me,
You hold me in Your arms.

THE BEST IS YET TO COME

When your world seems dim
And you feel all alone,
Turn to the Saviour
Upon His Throne.

All is not lost,
We have the "Light of the World"
Though life seems barren,
All is well.

He will never leave you,
He is by your side,
He will carry your weary heart,
While you wait for the turning tide.

Nothing stays the same forever,
Trust in His great love,
The future will unfold,
The best is yet to come.

The best is yet to come
If we sustain our love and more,
Use our trust and faith,
He will come with His rewards.

IN PERFECT COMMUNION

In perfect communion
With the Holy One,
When there are no distractions
Two become one.

In perfect communion
My thoughts fly to a higher place
Where my Saviour never leaves me,
He walks my daily pace.

In perfect communion
He is by my side,
Acceptance comes full circle
With a love to last all time.

In perfect communion
My trust comes to the test,
Sweetness flows between us,
I lay my head upon His breast.

In perfect communion
I give my heart to You,
Your gift of the Holy Spirit
Fills me with You!

KING OF MERCY

There is a King of Mercy
His reign will never end,
He came to earth to show us
How to live and to repent.

Without His Holy teaching
We could never understand,
Why we should try to forgive
The hurts from our fellowman.

His cry, "Father, forgive them
For they know not what they do",
In His time of suffering
The King of Mercy still loved you.

He cared so much for mankind,
He paid a debt we could never afford,
Because He is the King of Mercy
He cancelled the sin for one and all.

His name, is Jesus
And He loves you from Eternity,
Whatever wrong you have done in this life
A pardon, you will receive.

His angels will roar for you
When you carry mercy on your path,
A blessing beyond compare,
Now the King of Mercy, lives, in your heart.

EVERY DAY IS A NEW PAGE

Every day is a new page
When golden skies awake,
Light filters through my room
As I pray for the new day.

For whatever comes my way,
I have to keep an open mind,
Every day is a new page,
God will be my guide.

So take Him on your journey
Whether it be long or short,
Ask for His strength and knowledge
To power your every thought.

Pray for His loving hand
To steady you on your way,
You only have to ask Him,
Every day is a new page.

WHEN GOD MOVES THE SOUL

When the soul is moved by God,
Great things happen to the heart,
His Holy Spirit moves,
You will make a new start.

You will know divine love
In fullness so complete,
Your cup will overflow
At His Mercy Seat.

When God moves your soul
A new life begins,
You can't believe the change
That's happening within.

Your conscience will step forth
In faith and truth,
Your heart will reveal
A love that is brand new.

When God moves the soul
Wonders are revealed,
One to one with Jesus
Are moments so surreal.

When God moves the soul,
Heaven comes to stay,
Jesus lives within,
You are on your way.

MY JESUS

My Jesus is my Saviour,
Long ago He touched my life,
He opened my heart
To reveal His shining light.

My Jesus never leaves me,
He never tires of my requests,
His Spirit brings His love,
He's my Counsellor and Friend.

My Jesus is my Refuge,
He provides shelter and food,
He gathers me under His wings,
He stands for Grace and Truth.

I see Him in the sunrise,
Rolling seas and setting sun,
High majestic mountains,
Springtime colour brings His love.

My Jesus is my Lord,
He rules over Heaven and Earth,
Lover of my soul,
One day He will return.

My Jesus is my Shepherd,
"Hallowed" He'll always be,
My Saviour, Lord and Master,
The risen Christ for me!

PART THREE

"God said "I am who I am"…
This is my name forever; this is what
all future generations are to call me."

Exodus 3 : 14, 15

HIS CHURCH…
THE BODY OF CHRIST…

"I praise you, O Lord; teach me your ways."

Psalm 119 : 12

THE SPIRIT HEART

The Spirit heart moves quietly,
Wrapped in Spirit love,
A guidance that prompts and whispers
God's ways from above.

A knowing of His presence
Felt deep inside,
A real assurance
That with you He abides.

Fragrant notes of comfort
Just at the right time,
In your hour of need
The "Helper" will arrive.

An open heart of surrender
Bids Him come near,
His loving arms will hold you
As He takes any doubts and fears.

No mountain you can't climb,
No ford you can't cross,
No valley so deep
When the "Comforter" you lean upon.

The Spirit heart will shine
Of God's glory from within,
His sweetness pouring over you,
His light will never dim.

QUIET TIME TOGETHER

In this quiet time together
I call You to my side,
In the faith and love I feel
That I just can't hide.

Your presence so real
Because my heart tells me so,
A blessing so rich
From You, I know.

My thoughts are hushed
As the joy I feel
Wraps my whole being
As in reverence I kneel.

My Holy Redeemer
Holds me in awe,
In this quiet time
Our love grows more and more.

The dawn so fresh,
Coolness is sweet,
This quiet time so real
As we two meet.

This reassurance awakes
A peace unspeakable,
In union with the Spirit,
My heart is truly full.

LIVING WATERS

His living waters heal our hurts
With oil fragrant sweet,
Smoothing out the layers
With His love that's so complete.

His living waters shine like diamonds
In His light of love,
Sparkling every moment
In His realm above.

His living waters you can drink,
You'll never thirst again,
Forever in His Kingdom
If your heart you give to Him.

His living waters come
To wash you clean inside,
A moving of His Spirit
To open your heart wide.

His living waters flow
From His Heavenly Throne,
Where Father and Son abide
To bring you home.

Wonder and awe await
Far beyond your dreams,
Living waters flow for you
From His Throne in crystal streams.

REVELATION BREAKTHROUGH

Your heart revelation breakthrough
Is victory indeed,
The Holy Spirit takes His place,
God's precious Holy Seed.

A resurgence of the heart
Now it's open wide,
The Spirit's flame ignites
A love you just can't hide.

A feeling of cleansing
Now you've encountered God,
No chance meeting;
His wings you now ride upon.

Your revelation breakthrough,
In praise angels roar,
Your name is known in heaven,
In the Spirit's love you soar.

Such power and wonder you know,
A child of the Most High,
Your revelation breakthrough
Has forever changed your life!

YOUR SPIRIT IN ME LORD

Your Spirit in me Lord,
Such a special gift,
Always and forever
In my heart He will live.

He's changed the way I feel,
Turned the bitter into sweet,
The dark became light
When I said "I believe".

A never ending power
That urges me on,
A voice always prompting,
A love for which I long.

Your Spirit in me Lord
Came down from above,
So precious, He luminates
The love of God.

One of The Trinity,
All power, majesty and love,
My Comforter, Healer and Helper,
Acts by the Father above.

The Spirit in me,
Wonder and awe I know,
His peace and calm fills me,
That's why I love Him so!

PASSING THROUGH

I am but passing through
The stepping stones of life,
In accordance with the Spirit
Who leads me in The Light.

I am a child of God
Renewed and restored,
He's changed me on the inside
So it's Him I adore.

I am but passing through
Making way to Heaven's Door,
Though my path be steep and windy
From the call of earthly chores.

I keep my eyes on Heaven
As I walk in His Light,
He leads me on my journey
With His love that satisfies.

My eternal life is waiting
Further on and beyond,
I'm only passing through
But for now I must press on.

All will be revealed
On the day He returns,
For His Bride in waiting,
The believers of His Church.

AGELESS TIME...
WHERE HE ABIDES...

"There are many rooms in my Father's house, and I am going to prepare a place for you. I would not tell you this if it were not so. And after I go and prepare a place for you, I will come back and take you to myself, so that you will be where I am."

John 14 : 2, 3

MAKEOVER

He's longing for your invite
To call Him into your heart,
So He can start your makeover
And bring you out of the dark.

He loves the sound of your voice
In praise, worship and prayer,
He will listen forever
Because for you He cares.

No request is too big,
No question too long,
His answer will come in His time
Because to Him you belong.

He has rewards that are waiting
For you to unwrap and use,
Manifested in Heaven
As He works on the new you.

Your makeover so special,
Straight from His Heavenly Throne,
A gift when His Spirit arrives in your heart
You now have a place in His home.

Your makeover from the Divine,
No finer work you will see,
Through His grace and mercy,
The image of Him you will be!

PEARLS OF LIGHT

Listen to your soul
For inward peace,
Reach for God's Word
To feel complete.

The challenges of life
Will weigh on your mind
But if you seek God's help,
Pearls of light you will find.

Your actions will reflect
How you feel inside,
Within His pearls of light
With you He will reside.

Look into your soul
It reveals the truth,
It holds His pearls of light
That His Spirit brings to you.

Look into your soul
That holds His pearls of light,
They will reflect on your heart
To make your life so bright!

THE VOICE IN ME

Lord, I've found a voice in me
In many different ways,
It's Your Spirit I hear
As You live in me each day.

I feel so blessed
To be prompted this way,
When I listen to His voice
My fears just run away.

He lays on my heart
A conscious thought,
Or brings someone to mind
Who needs the prayer You taught.

His Baptism of love
That flows over me,
Brings Your power and grace
That leads me to "believe".

He shows me Your ways
In great magnitude,
I love Him so dearly,
Holy Spirit sent by You!

UNTARNISHED LOVE

Nothing can tarnish the love
Of Jesus Christ my Lord,
Accepting Him into my heart
Together we are one accord.

I refuse to let this love pale
On days that seem so dim,
No matter how I'm feeling
I must keep my eyes on Him.

Though dark shadows cross my path
His light still shines on me,
To reveal His guiding hand
That will lead me to Eternity.

In love we rejoice together
In adoration I fall to my knees,
Our love will never tarnish
In all Eternity.

THE FIRST HOLY SEED

Jesus Christ our Lord,
The first Holy Seed,
Together with the Father
Called Creation to be.

From His heavenly realm
He called the open seas,
He spoke to the mountains,
The first Holy Seed.

He called for the rivers
And the valleys deep,
He put in place the forests,
The first Holy Seed.

He smoothed the desert sands
And called life in the sea,
He made the Sun and Moon,
The first Holy Seed.

But His greatest creation
Was the birth of you and me,
He made us in His image,
The first Holy Seed.

Creators of time
All power over heaven and earth,
The first Holy seed
Came to earth to serve.

A LONGING IN THE HEART

There's a longing in the heart
That just won't go away,
It's the love of the Lord
In your heart has made its way.

A joy beyond words
You can't explain,
A contentment so real,
God's perfection displayed.

A peace fills your being
You don't understand,
So pure and divine
From God's Holy Hand.

There's a longing in the heart
For a meeting divine,
To see Him face to face,
The One True Vine.

All will be revealed
In His time soon enough
When that longing in your heart
Will be given up.

Dwelling in His presence
For all eternity,
Joy beyond this world
When the Saviour you see!

PART FOUR

"Now my heart is troubled – and what shall I say?
Shall I say, "Father, do not let this hour come upon me"?
But that is why I came – so that I might go through this
hour of suffering. Father, bring glory to your name!"
Then a voice spoke from heaven, "I have brought
glory to it, and I will do so again."

John 12 : 27 - 28

JESUS SACRIFICIAL LOVE ...
BROUGHT SUFFERING AND SACRIFICE...

"At noon the whole country was covered with
darkness, which lasted for three hours. At three
o'clock Jesus cried out with a loud shout,
"Eloi, Eloi, lema sabachthani?" which means,
"My God, my God, why did you abandon me?"...
"With a loud cry Jesus died."
"The curtain hanging in the Temple was torn in two,
from top to bottom."

Mark 15 : 33, 34, 37, 38

IN THE SHADOWS OF GETHSEMANE

Passover dawn awakes,
A promise from long ago,
A prophecy fulfilled,
To Gethsemane the Saviour will go.

A betrayal on the horizon
Had no reprieve,
Set now in motion
In the shadows of Gethsemane.

Bewilderment unleashed
On the chosen few,
How can this be?
Only the Saviour knew.

In the shadows of Gethsemane
Soldiers came to bind
The one so precious,
No sin in Him to find.

His beloved now scattered,
Feared for their lives,
One life for many
Gave the gift of eternal life.

In the shadows of Gethsemane
In the dark of night,
The Lamb of God gave
For you and me, His life.

ABSOLUTION

Wherever you are with Jesus
He's longing for you
To give Him some time
Because He died on the Cross for you.

The one on the other side
Of Jesus at Calvary
Was given absolution
Because in Jesus he believed.

The Saviour's precious blood
Flowed that day
To give us absolution
And wash our sin away.

No more will it be remembered,
The Lord in His Word promised this,
Salvation was born,
Absolution for our sin.

Absolution for the world
When lips truly confess,
"The Savior died for me
Now He lives in Heaven's rest."

Absolution was granted
For the one on the other side,
His faith saved Him,
Jesus promised him Paradise!

IN THE SHADOWS OF THE OLIVE GROVE

The reason for His birth
Was a pending sacrifice,
Now approaching fast
For the sins of all mankind.

In the shadows of the Olive Grove
Weary eyes surrender to sleep,
While the Master close-by
Prayed so earnestly.

In the shadows of the Olive Grove
Soldiers came in search,
To bind the Lamb of God
For a pouch of silvers worth.

A kiss would reveal
His Ministry now complete,
The Lamb's Sacrifice
Would take Him to Calvary.

In the shadows of the Olive Grove
He held the world in His hands,
Our redemption was nigh,
A Cross would claim the Son of Man.

FATHER GOD RAISED HIM ...
TO LIFE ON THE THIRD DAY...

"Suddenly there was a violent earthquake; an angel of the Lord came down from heaven, rolled the stone away, and sat on it. His appearance was like lightning, and his clothes were white as snow...The angel spoke to the women. "You must not be afraid," he said. "I know you are looking for Jesus, who was crucified. He is not here; he has been raised, just as he said"...

Matthew 28 : 2, 3, 5, 6

REUNION

Reunion so special,
The stone was rolled away,
The Saviour was raised,
It was Easter Day.

Reunion with the Father
After the darkness of Calvary,
Scriptures prophesied,
He will rise in Victory.

The Father gave Him great glory
By raising Him to life,
A miracle only by God
Overturning darkness to Light.

A reunion so special
Father God and Holy Son,
Returning to the Throne,
The battle over death is won.

Now in Heaven's splendour
Father and Son sit side by side,
Majestic wonder all around,
Forever they will abide.

Their reunion now eternal
In Heaven they abide,
The darkness of Calvary
Gives way for Paradise.

GOOD ENOUGH FOR A PARDON

Are we good enough for a pardon Lord?
Our shame brings its doubts,
But You are love itself Lord
That's what Calvary was about.

Are we good enough for a pardon Lord?
Our guilt surely says "no",
But by the will of the Heavenly Father
A young Nazarene thought so!

He took our sin to Calvary,
It was His Father's call,
He was nailed to a wooden Cross,
He bore the sin of all.

Yes, the Son of God came to earth
For that one day at Calvary,
So we could have eternal life
And a pardon to receive!

For a pardon for every sin
We only have to believe,
He died on the Cross for us
And was raised to victory!

HEART OF HEARTS

CHRIST'S BIRTH BROUGHT GREAT... JOY, PEACE AND HOPE...

"The angel said to her, "Don't be afraid, Mary; God has been gracious to you. You will become pregnant and give birth to a son, and you will name him Jesus. He will be great and will be called the Son of the Most High God."...

Luke 1 : 30 - 32

NEW BORN KING

The royal line of David
Evolved from a line of Kings,
Descendants from Abraham
Who brought the Prince of Peace.

This line of royalty
Has passed through centuries,
All in God's appointed time
The Messiah we would see.

The glorious Star of the East,
A guide for the Magi to bring
Gifts of Frankincense, Myrrh and Gold
To the precious new-born King.

They would name Him "Jesus",
The Name above all names,
God's gift to all mankind,
"Blessed" He will remain.

He will be all Humility,
He will save mankind from sin,
This Lord of Lords, our Saviour,
The everlasting King of Kings.

This royal line of David,
A birthright of Kings,
Forever will hold majesty,
Glory to the new-born King!

IN AWE SHE HELD HIM

In awe she held Him,
Born that Holy Night,
In wonder and majesty,
The Star above shone bright.

Heavenly angels rejoiced
In unison they sang,
Glory to the Lord,
He is the Holy Lamb.

In awe she held Him,
The newborn Holy Christ,
Wrapped in swaddling clothes,
The world's Shining Light.

Now golden dawn awakes,
Orange sweeps the sky,
Glory fills the stable,
God's precious Son arrived.

In awe she held Him;
Born the King of Kings,
He lives forever more,
Salvation to the world He brings!

MESSIAH BORN IN THE STABLE

Christmas brings faith
From the first Holy Night,
The Messiah born in the stable,
He's now our Shining Light!

What joy He brought,
No words can explain,
Messiah born in the stable,
It was Christmas Day.

Christmas Day brings wonder,
Awe, peace and joy,
Messiah born in the stable,
God's Newborn Baby Boy!

The Magi came with gifts,
They knew the stars above,
They followed the brightest one
Leading them to God's Newborn Son.

Holy, Holy Night,
The Saviour has arrived,
Humbly born in a stable,
He came to bring eternal life.

Holy, Glorious Night,
Power and Majesty Divine,
Christ born in the stable,
That first Christmas night.

A PRICELESS LIFE

He was born under
The Star from the East
And the wonder of angels
Who declared His birth in peace.

The shepherds in the fields
Saw this glorious sight
Of the angels who told them
Of His birth that night.

He would grow into a man
Who could walk on the sea,
He could touch and heal,
This man from Galilee.

Down through the ages
This priceless life stands out,
His awe and His wonder
We cannot live without.

One priceless life,
Called "The Nazarene",
One so perfect
Will again be seen!

ALSO BY CLAIRE GROSE

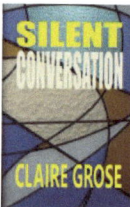 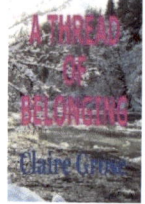 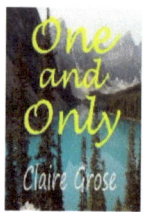

  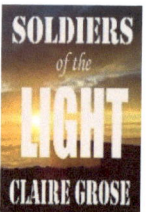

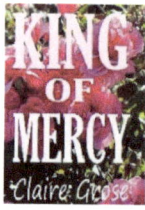  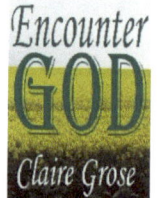

ABOUT THE AUTHOR

Claire worked as a Government Public Servant in the Lands Department, Adelaide, South Australia until she married and became a mother of two boys.

She later returned to the work force during which time she gained a "Living Hope" Phone Counselling certificate which influenced her need to help others.

Through this and personal experience she found herself inspired by God's love to put pen to paper.

PHOTO CREDITS

COVER PHOTO: Salisbury Uniting Church; S.A. – Claire Grose

Page 2: Salisbury Uniting Church; S.A. - Claire Grose
Page 12: Pink Super Moon; S.A. – Joshua Woskett
Page 24: Lavendar Garden; S.A. – Lynne
Page 31: Autumn Leaves; Barossa Valley – Claire Grose
Page 39: Barossa Palm Trees; S.A. – Claire Grose
Page 47: Fremont Park; S.A. - Claire Grose
Page 55: Chain of Hearts; Qld – Carol and Den
Page 70: Salisbury Uniting Church; S.A. – Claire Grose
Page 78: Salisbury Uniting Church; S.A – Claire Grose
Page 87: Garden Tomb, Jerusalem; Israel – Dennis and Carol
Page 92: Salisbury Uniting Church; S.A – Claire Grose
Page 96: Salisbury Uniting Church; S.A. – Claire Grose

HEART OF HEARTS

www.ingramcontent.com/pod-product-compliance
Lightning Source LLC
Chambersburg PA
CBHW042043290426
44109CB00001B/14